Jay Triano

foreword by **Steve Nash**

HOW TO
PLAY LIKE
THE PROS

BASKETBALL
BASICS

GREYSTONE BOOKS

D&M PUBLISHERS INC.

Vancouver/Toronto/Berkeley

*This book is dedicated to those youth who aspire to be better
at anything they do. Most important, this book is dedicated to
my children, Courtney, Jessi, and Dustin. Their drive
and determination to become better at all of their disciplines
motivates me to continue to learn, teach, and coach.*

JAY TRIANO

Greystone Books
A division of D&M Publishers Inc.
2323 Quebec Street, Suite 201
Vancouver BC Canada V5T 4S7
www.greystonebooks.com

PHOTO CREDITS
Instructional photographs by Alastair Bird

Professional player photos supplied by
National Basketball Association/Getty Images:
individiual photographers:
Front cover: David Sandford · p. 4: Barry Gossage
p. 6, p. 46: Ron Turenne · p. 10: Cameron Browne
p. 20: Sam Forencich · p. 22: Ned Dishman
p. 34: Gary Dineen · p. 66: Joe Murphy
p. 56: John Biever/Sports Illustrated/Getty Images
p. 72: Nick LahamGetty Images

Library and Archives Canada Cataloguing in Publication
Triano, Jay, 1958–
Basketball basics : how to play like the pros / Jay Triano ; foreword by Steve Nash.
ISBN 978-1-55365-451-3

1. Basketball—Training—Juvenile literature. 2. Basketball for children—Training. I. Title.
GV885.35.T75   2009 j796.323'2   C2008-906502-6

Editing by Michelle Benjamin
Copy editing by Anne Rose
Cover and interior design by Peter Cocking
Printed and bound in China by C&C Offset Printing Co. Ltd.
Printed on acid-free paper
Distributed in the U.S. by Publishers Group West

We gratefully acknowledge the financial support of the Canada Council for the Arts,
the British Columbia Arts Council, the Province of British Columbia through the Book
Publishing Tax Credit, and the Government of Canada through the Book Publishing
Industry Development Program (BPIDP) for our publishing activities.

Also, our thanks to NIKE, for providing balls, shoes, and uniforms to the young players at
our photo shoot. And thanks to Stephen McGilligan for putting together an All-Star team.

CONTENTS

BASKETBALL IS the greatest game. When I started playing as a young boy, I was obsessive. I took a basketball with me everywhere I went, and I practised dribbling and shooting for hours every day. That's still the best way to become a better player. Use every opportunity you have to practise the fundamental skills. Dedicate yourself to working every day on your footwork, your ball handling and dribbling, your passing and catching, your shooting and rebounding. I also believe it's important to practise each position, offensive and defensive, and to always know what to look for when you're on the court.

But remember that basketball is not just a lot of hard work. It's also tremendous fun, and it's a fantastic way to stay fit and healthy. A pick-up game with your friends makes a good workout. And playing other sports and being involved in physical activity will help make you an even better player. When I'm not on a basketball court, you can often find me playing soccer with my family or riding my bike.

Don't forget to be a good sport, and be respectful of your teammates and coaches, as well as your opponents. Teamwork is as important as individual talent. And be humble. Remember that no matter how good you are or how much you know, there's always more to learn and always someone better than you who can teach you something.

It's also important to be a good and responsible person. When you're not playing ball, make sure you're helping out your family, your friends, and your community. Get out there and work for positive social change, for peace, for your planet.

Jay Triano is one of the best coaches in the game. His support played a big role in my development, and his guidance helped me become the skilled and disciplined player I am today. Follow Jay's advice in *Basketball Basics,* and commit to learning the skills and practising the drills that he provides, and I guarantee you'll be a stronger player. Because if you want to improve your basketball skills, there are three things you should keep with you at all times: your love for the game, your basketball, and Jay Triano's *Basketball Basics.*

STEVE NASH

1 GETTING READY

SMART ATHLETES commit themselves to a regular warm-up routine, with stretching exercises before every game and practice. Skilled basketball players must also be flexible, which means all of their joints and muscles should have a wide range of motion. You need a complete stretching and warm-up program to make this happen. And if you follow it regularly, you will improve your play, increase your quickness, agility, and balance, and prevent injuries.

"Always work hard. Basically that's what it's about. Outworking the other person and always believing in yourself. You have to keep your dream alive."
< CHRIS BOSH

Each exercise that follows is designed to work on a specific part of your body. Remember: it is important to warm up before every game and practice. A proper warm-up includes all of the activities on the following pages.

Warming Up & Stretching

Morgan's back is straight and she pumps her arms as she drives her knees to hip level.

As Diane's heel makes contact, she quickly kicks back to the floor and switches legs.

Dustin's arms and legs are straight as he rotates from the hip.

PRO TIP The first thing we want to do when we get into the gym is grab a basketball and start dribbling and shooting. But by warming up and stretching first we allow our bodies to get ready to perform at a higher level. Increasing your flexibility will help you to become a better player.

HIGH KNEES Stand up tall with your back straight, your chest up and out. Take high steps, driving alternating knees up to hip level. Land on the balls of your feet and get one knee up again as soon as your opposite foot lands. Make sure your feet have minimal contact with the floor. Pump your arms as you drive your knees up.

HEEL TO BUTT Stand up tall with your back straight, your chest up and out. Bend one leg at the knee so the heel of your foot makes contact with the bottom of your butt, then kick it back to the floor quickly and switch to the other leg. Land on the balls of your feet and move explosively.

TOE TOUCH Stand with your arms out to the sides at shoulder height. Keep your arms and legs as straight as possible as you kick up from the hip, rotating to touch your toes to your opposite hand. You should feel the stretch in your hamstrings. This is good balance-training for the support leg. If you're doing this exercise right, it will look like you are doing the cancan dance step.

Warming Up & Stretching

Zach can feel the stretch in his leg muscles as he pulls his knee to his chest.

In Gord's lunge, he holds his forward knee at a 90-degree angle.

KNEE TO CHEST Stand up tall with your back straight, your chest up and out. Bring one knee to your chest, then grab your leg just below the knee with one hand and just above the ankle with the other. Squeeze your leg toward your chest—you should feel the stretch in your leg muscles. Make sure you are stable and balanced on your standing foot. Squeeze for 1 or 2 seconds before taking a step forward and alternating legs.

LUNGE Put your hands behind your head, elbows out. Take a step forward with one leg, keeping your chest high and your back straight. Your front knee should not go past your front foot and your knee bend should be at 90 degrees. Your back knee should be down, so that a straight vertical line could be drawn from that knee and through your hip, shoulder, and ear. Your lower leg should be parallel with the floor. Hold for 3 to 5 seconds, then switch legs.

PRO TIP Improper warm up and stretching can lead to injury or soreness. Make sure to breathe through your stretches. Remember: after a hard practice or workout it's important to cool down and stretch the same way that you did at the beginning of your workout.

CONDITIONING

YOU MUST be in good physical shape to be a skilled athlete. Some think that big arms and shoulders are the key to being strong. But an athlete's true strength is measured by how fit and solid he or she is in the abdominal area, also known as your "core." Every athletic movement starts from the centre of your body. A regular conditioning routine will help you move quickly and stay in control.

When you hold the basketball in your core area—directly in front of your body, between your shoulders and knees—you have the most control and strength. If you extend the ball too far away from your body, outside your core area, you will limit how well you perform essential basketball skills.

Three key elements ensure a safe and successful workout:

1 Keep your stomach tight.

2 Keep your back straight.

3 Don't forget to breathe!

Most of the following core-strength exercises use an exercise ball. Remember: it's important to warm up and stretch before starting your core-strength session.

> "You can never think you learned it all in life— there is always something else coming. That is the same with basketball. You can always work on your game and be a better player and person."
> ‹ **DIRK NOWITZKI**

Core-Strengthening Exercises

Daniel's back is straight and both feet are flat on the floor. His stomach muscles are tight as he tilts his pelvis (left) and rotates his hips in both directions (right).

Jordan's back is straight as he turns from his hips and rotates his shoulders from one side to the other.

PRO TIP The core is the centre of all your athletic movement. The more you can develop and strengthen it, the better you will be able to move.

PELVIS TILT Sit up tall on the exercise ball, with your back straight and both feet flat on the floor. Tilt your pelvis forward, then back, keeping your stomach muscles tight.

HIP CIRCLE Sit up tall on the exercise ball, with your back straight and both feet flat on the floor. Rotate your hips in a clockwise direction. Do two complete circles, then another two in a counter-clockwise direction.

SUPERMAN Lie face down on the exercise ball. Balance on your hips, with your feet and hands touching the floor to stabilize you. Raise your right arm straight out in front and your left leg straight out in back. Tighten the muscles in your back, butt, and shoulders and hold for 2 seconds. Switch sides and repeat.

BACK ROTATION Lie with your shoulder blades on the ball, legs forward, together, and bent at the knees, feet on the floor. A line drawn between your shoulders, hips, and knees would be parallel with the floor. Then, with your arms straight up and hands together, roll onto one shoulder. Your fingers should point in the direction that you're rolling in. Return to centre, then rotate onto the other shoulder, with your hands and arms pointing in the other direction.

Core-Strengthening Exercises

Daniel keeps his back straight as rolls his shoulders back and forth across the ball.

Dustin concentrates on his balance and uses his core strength to roll forward while doing his "prayers."

SUPINE LATERAL ROLL "Supine" means "lying on your back." Lie with your upper back and shoulders on the ball, your knees bent and your feet flat on the floor. Keeping your back straight, roll your upper back and shoulders across the ball. The supine lateral roll, like many other exercise-ball moves, is more about balance and stability than strength.

PRAYERS Get on your knees facing the ball, then lean forward. Place your forearms on the ball to balance yourself, keeping your palms together. Then roll onto the ball, lifting your knees off the floor. Keep your back straight and your stomach in. Extend your arms out in front of you, keeping your palms together, while using your core strength to keep your body in a straight line. Repeat.

FLOOR CRUNCH Lie on your back on the floor, with knees bent and feet flat. Cross your hands across your chest. Roll your shoulders up and off the floor, keeping your arms against your chest, and touch your elbows to your knees.

PRO TIP Use the exercise ball any and all the time. It helps with stability and posture. Do your homework sitting on the ball, or watch TV. Repeating different movements and positions on the ball will help develop your core.

Core-Strengthening Exercises

In this ski tuck, Zach keeps his spine straight and his arms fully extended.

Jordan holds his back straight and concentrates on balance and his core muscles.

Morgan's arms and legs are fully extended in the V-sit-up.

PRO TIP Try dribbling a basketball or playing catch while doing different types of balancing moves on the ball. Not only will this help your basketball skills, it will also help develop your core strength and your balance—and it's fun.

SKI TUCK Lie face down with your feet on the ball behind you, hands on the floor, arms in a push-up position. Roll your knees toward your chest, then roll back out to the starting position. Tuck your knees in and extend your back out quickly. Keep your spine straight—don't let your lower back sag.

SIT ON THE BALL Sit on the ball with your arms out to the side for balance, feet off the floor. Hold the position for as long as possible. Keep your back straight. If you can balance for more than one minute, have a partner pass you a basketball while you're sitting on the exercise ball. Try to pass it back.

KNEEL ON THE BALL Kneel on the ball for as long as possible, keeping your back straight. Remember: you're working on balance and core strength.

V-SIT-UP Lie on your back with arms fully extended over your head. Lift both legs and both arms and touch your toes to your fingers by bending at the waist. Lower your arms and legs simultaneously.

Foot Quickness Exercises

Zach keeps his back straight as he quickly alternates toe-taps on the bench.

You have to be fast to play basketball, which means having quick feet *and* being able to run speedily up and down the court. Do you understand the difference? Some people are built with natural speed. But everyone is able to improve how quickly they can move their feet, which means they can make more effective basketball plays. Exercises to increase foot quickness will help your movement on the basketball floor by strengthening your lower legs and ankles. These drills are easy to learn. Challenge yourself to do them as fast as possible.

ALTERNATING TOE-TAP ON BENCH Stand in front of a bench with one foot on the floor, the other on the edge of the bench. Quickly switch feet. Keep your body tall and straight, but look down a little to keep sight of the bench. Your feet should move quickly, with minimal contact with the floor or the bench. Land on the balls of your feet. See how many sets you can do in 30 seconds. As you improve, see how many you can do in a minute.

PRO TIP As with any other skill, the best way to increase your foot quickness is to practise. Jump back and forth over a line, or tap your feet as fast as possible. To be good at doing any movement quickly, you have to practise doing it quickly.

Foot Quickness Exercises

Zach quickly steps up with his left foot, then his right, then down with his left, and down with his right.

Diane launches up and over the bench with both feet, landing gently and immediately jumping up and over again.

PRO TIP An important part of having quick feet is being on your toes—literally. Any jump or quick move will be more effective if you are on your toes. The expression "stay on your toes" means, "be ready to move and react." When we say, "don't get caught flat-footed" we mean "don't be slow and unprepared."

ONE-TWO TOUCH AND DOWN Stand in front of a bench with both feet on the floor. Step up with your left foot, quickly followed by your right foot. Step down just as quickly, left foot first, followed by your right, then repeat. This should be a quick upward and downward movement. Count "one" when both feet have touched the bench and returned to the floor. On the second set, lead with the opposite foot. See how many sets you can do in 30 seconds. See how many you can do in a minute.

SKI JUMP Stand sideways to the bench. With your feet together, jump up and over the bench, landing on the other side on the balls of your feet. Then, as soon as your feet make contact with the floor, quickly jump back to the other side. When you're in the air, your knees should be tucked up toward your hips. See how many sets you can do in 30 seconds. See how many you can do in a minute. This exercise can also be done by jumping side to side over a line on the court.

Jumping Exercises

Matthew jumps with both feet together, lands gently, then launches himself immediately up onto the second box.

Jordan pushes off explosively with his inside foot on the bench, then lands gently with his opposite foot on the bench.

Great basketball players can jump high. High jumpers finish closer to the basket, challenge shots, and get rebounds. And though all players like to think about dunking the ball, you have to be able to get up and over the rim to do it. Jumping drills, along with foot-quickness exercises, increase leg strength and explosive power, and improve your ability to get up to the net.

TWO-BOX JUMP Place two boxes or benches 3 feet (1 metre) apart—one should be higher than the other by about 1.5–2 feet (40–60 centimetres). Stand on the edge of the lower box, jump off, and land gently on the floor on both feet. As soon as you land, jump up onto the second box. Remember: explode upward and drive your knees to your chest, and land as softly as possible on top of the second box.

BENCH PUSH-OFF Stand beside a bench. Place your inside foot on top of the bench, holding your body straight and tall. Push up with that inside foot, jumping up and sideways so that you land on the other side of the bench—with your opposite foot now on top of the bench and your "inside" foot now on the floor, on the outside. Repeat, concentrating on landing and pushing off again as quickly as possible.

PRO TIP The best way to be a better jumper is to practise jumping. Challenge yourself to jump up and reach for different objects or marks on a wall. It's like reaching for your goals. Once you get there, reach for something higher.

Four-Corner Conditioning Drill

PROGRESSIONS

- As you return to the centre cone, have your coach yell out which cone to run to next.
- Change the direction of the turns around each outside cone.
- Increase the distance of the outside cones from the centre to about 13 feet (4 metres). Then:
- Dribble a basketball while running the drill, always facing one direction.
- Dribble a tennis ball while running the drill, always facing one direction.

FOUR-CORNER DRILL FACING ONE DIRECTION Set up four cones in a diamond shape. Put one cone in the centre of the diamond and each of the other cones about 8 feet (2.5 metres) from this centre cone. Stand at the centre cone in an athletic stance, facing one direction. (Remember: you will face this same direction throughout the entire drill.) Run to the cone in front of you, circle around it, then back-pedal to the centre. Without stopping, loop around the centre cone and shuffle sideways to the right-side cone. Circle around that cone, then shuffle sideways back to the centre cone. Circle around the centre cone, then back-pedal to the rear cone. Run back to centre. Shuffle sideways to the left-side cone, then shuffle back to centre.

Basketball Stance

Diane is well balanced, with her knees bent and her head up.

Zach holds the ball close to his core, in the most protected area and where he has the most strength.

The basketball stance is the basic, or "ready," athletic position that allows you to move quickly as well as shoot, pass, catch, or dribble without repositioning your body. In a proper basketball stance, you are well balanced and low, with knees bent and feet at least shoulder-width apart. Lean slightly forward, keeping your head up and eyes ahead. Your free arm should be waist-high. Your elbow is bent, working to either protect or dig for the ball. You use this stance in every aspect of the game—on offense and defense, and when dribbling, catching, passing, and preparing to shoot.

PRO TIP To really understand the difference between a low stance and high stance, ask a partner to push on your shoulders when you are crouched low, and then again when you are standing high. In which position are you more stable?

PLAYING OFFENSE

STRONG OFFENSE wins games. An offensive player's most important goal is to move the ball up the court and into the basket. To do this, the ball is advanced either by dribbling or by passing to a teammate, but the aim is always to get the ball to a player who is in position to score. Ball control, dribbling, passing, and shooting are key skills for every offensive player. Perfect these skills and you will be a valuable member of your team. Proper stance is also important.

You always have the advantage when you are on offense because you know where you are going and what you are going to do next, while the defense has to read and react to your moves. Make sure you use this advantage!

"My dream is to play against the best players in the world."
< **RUDY FERNANDEZ**

BALL HANDLING

BALL HANDLING is key to being a good basketball player, and dribbling is the most important ball-handling skill. How do you become a better ball handler? You keep a basketball with you at all times, and you dribble that ball everywhere you go. Dribble your basketball to school and dribble it home again. Dribble it up and down the stairs. Dribble it on grass and on pavement, in the snow and when it's raining. If you can dribble a ball in all kinds of conditions, imagine how easy it will be to dribble on smooth hardwood. The more a ball is with you the more control you will develop. A good player can dribble with both hands, at various speeds, and in all directions.

"I love setting goals and I love having obstacles... I feel happy that my teammates have the confidence in me to put the ball in my hands."
< **CANDACE PARKER**

Stationary Ball Handling

Jordan uses the pads of his fingers to tap the ball from one hand to the other.

Jordan keeps his eyes forward as he moves the ball in a figure-8 around his legs.

Dustin stays in the basketball stance as he orbits the ball around his waist.

Handling a basketball while standing still and not dribbling helps you develop a feel for the ball. It will also develop your hand-eye coordination, as well as your hand strength and quickness.

Control the ball with the pads of your fingers—not the tips of your fingers and not the palm of your hand. Remember: the wider you spread your fingers, the more of the ball your hand will cover, giving you even more control.

- With your arms straight, tap or pat the ball from one hand to the other. Do this out in front of your chest, over your head, and down below your waist. Make sure your arms are straight, and keep focused on your wrists and the pads of your finger. The ball never touches the floor.

- Move the ball in an orbit around different parts of your body: under your arms, around your waist, your head, your legs, etc. Move the ball in both directions, and change the height of the ball. Move the ball around your legs at knee level, in and out in a figure-8 pattern. Don't let the ball hit the floor.

Basic Dribble

Dustin is in his basketball stance, with one hand protecting the ball.

Ethan keeps control of the ball as he bounces close to the floor, then gradually moves up to shoulder height.

The better you can dribble a basketball, the better a player you will be. A strong dribbler can move quickly into position to make a play. Dribbling can also get you out of trouble if the defense is pressuring you, and it can help you get control of the ball or stop you from travelling and turning the ball over. One quick dribble can often put you in a better position to take a shot.

- Get into your basketball stance: head up and knees bent, with one hand dribbling and your other hand at a 90-degree angle in front of your body, protecting the ball. Keep the ball close to your core, where you have the most strength and control. Get the ball back up off the floor as quickly as possible. Keep your eyes forward. Don't look at the ball—your hands should always know where the ball is.

- Dribble the ball in place, bending your elbow and moving your entire arm on each bounce. The goal is to keep the ball in your hand as long as possible. Dribble as close to the floor as you can, then gradually move up to where you are pounding the ball from a standing-up position.

PRO TIP When doing simple ball-handling drills, challenge yourself by keeping your head up and not looking at the ball. Speed up until you are moving the ball as fast as you can.

Basic Dribble

Dustin dribbles back and forth in front of his body. His free hand is protecting the ball and his eyes look forward.

Matthew keeps his hand on the ball for as long as possible as he dribbles backward and forward beside his body.

PRO TIP Practise your dribbling skills as much with your left hand as with your right. Don't let your defender know which is your strong hand.

• Still in your stance, bounce the ball back and forth in front of your body, using one hand. Then bounce the ball forward and backward beside your body. The ball should look like a pendulum moving in an even rhythm in front of you, then beside you. When you've got control, increase your speed and change the height of the ball. Forward and backward dribbles and side-to-side dribbles will help you avoid the hands of defenders who will be looking to steal.

Remember: the better you can handle the ball in any situation, the better player you will be, regardless of your position. The more you work on your basic dribble, the more you will not have to look at the ball, and so you will be able to see your defenders and the floor. Practise dribbling a basketball while doing everyday things—walking to school, brushing your teeth, running up and down the stairs. The more the ball is a part of your hand, the less you have to think about dribbling, and the more you can be looking for defensive weaknesses in your opponents.

Speed Dribble

Dustin pushes the ball forward from shoulder height as he sprints after the ball.

The speed dribble is used on a fast break, on a turnover, and any time that you are accelerating away from a defender.

- Push the ball out in front of you and chase after it. The faster you run, the farther ahead you push the ball—while keeping control of it. To practise, start at a slow jog, then gradually pick up speed until you are running as fast as you can. Keep the ball away from your feet.

- The ball should bounce high in a speed dribble, even up to shoulder height, so that you have time to move your feet while the ball is in the air. Remember: your fingers are spread out and the pads of your fingers are controlling the ball.

- How many dribbles does it take for you to get from half-court into a layup? Try to get it down to 3 bounces.

PRO TIP When practising the speed dribble, your goal is to run as fast as you can—even at an all-out sprint—while dribbling the ball.

Crossover Dribble

Jordan prepares for a crossover dribble by protecting the ball with his free hand...

...which becomes his ball hand after a quick bounce.

He launches himself in the opposite direction and past his defender.

PRO TIP Any time you change direction, change your speed as well. Always accelerate as you move away from the defender. Stay low, and keep your shoulders lower than your defender's shoulders.

The crossover dribble is an excellent way to change direction and get past a defender. You bounce the ball to pass it—or cross over—from one hand to the other. The bounce should be quick and as close to your body as possible. The hand that was protecting becomes the receiving hand—ready to control the ball. Keep your head up and your back straight, knees bent. Lean slightly forward from your waist.

• When you pass the ball from one hand to the other, make sure you are still protecting it. Keep it close to your body and away from the defender. You want to get the ball to the floor and back up to your other hand as quickly as possible.

• As you pass the ball between hands, change direction with your feet and body. When the ball passes from your right to your left hand, plant your right foot hard, so that it becomes the push-off foot and you can accelerate in the opposite direction.

Behind-the-Back Dribble

Zach needs to protect the ball, so he moves it behind his back.

He keeps it close to his body and gets it down to the floor and back up quickly.

He's now open and able to speed off in the opposite direction.

If your defender is close, it can be dangerous to use the crossover dribble to change direction. Instead, use your body to protect the ball with a behind-the-back dribble. Keep your head up, your knees bent, and lean slightly forward.

- Face forward and get in your basketball stance. To get the ball behind your back, you will have to move it outside of your core. If the ball is in your right hand, move that hand back and to the right so that you can bounce the ball behind you and get it around your body. (Remember: do not let the ball get too far away from your body. If you pat your butt as you release the ball, it should mean that you're keeping the ball in close.) Next, plant your right foot and change direction, just like you did in the crossover dribble. Your left hand switches from protecting the ball to receiving. As soon as you catch the ball, get it back close to your core. Remember: the goal is to get the ball off the floor and back into your other hand as fast as possible. The receiving hand must be ready: fingers spread and elbow bent.

- Change direction, with the ball and your feet, using your legs to protect the ball from the defender. As you move the ball behind your back, plant your foot to change direction. The leg opposite from the hand you are dribbling with should come between you and your defender.

PRO TIP You only have control of the ball when it is in your hands. When you go behind your back with a dribble, you must get the ball into your other hand as fast as possible.

Between-the-Legs Dribble

Ethan wants to protect the ball from his defender.

He takes a long step forward and quickly bounces the ball between his legs.

He picks up the ball with his other hand and launches himself in the opposite direction.

PRO TIP Often, a player will dribble between his or her legs to make a flashy play, but this move is best used to protect the ball and get it to your other hand.

The between-the-legs dribble is usually a protection move, and is used in two ways. First, it allows you to accelerate forward past the defense while protecting the ball from a defender. Second, you can move the ball backward between your legs and into your other hand, away from a defender.

FORWARD: Take a long step forward, either toward the basket or past your defender, and then bounce the ball ahead, between your legs. Catch the ball with your opposite hand. This gives you forward momentum and also transfers the ball to the other side of your body.

BACKWARD: Bounce the ball backward between your legs for a protection dribble, centering the ball directly between your feet. Do not take a step forward, and be careful to not hit a leg or foot. If you are being closely guarded, this dribble allows you to get the ball into a strong position for either protecting or attacking.

Inside-Out Dribble

Dustin stops quickly and fakes right.

He launches himself quickly in the opposite direction, past his defender.

He keeps control of the ball and moves fast with a long stride.

The inside-out dribble—also called "stop-and-go"—is usually used on an open court and at high speed. It involves a quick stop and a change of direction, and is used to get a defender to move one way so that you can accelerate past.

- Throw off your defender by using a head fake: move your head and shoulders in one direction, then quickly run in the opposite direction. Keep the ball in one hand, move it in the same direction as your head and shoulders, then quickly plant the opposite foot and move the ball—and your head and shoulders—in the direction you really intend to go.

- Stand up straight, because you will be moving fast. This play is similar to the crossover dribble, but the ball never leaves the hand you are dribbling with. Change the direction of the bounce by moving your hand from one side of the ball to the other.

PRO TIP   The most important thing with the inside-out dribble is to sell your movement in one direction using the ball, your head and your shoulders, and then bring them all back in the opposite direction.

Back-Up Dribble

Diane stays low as she dribbles back and away from her defender.

When her defender stands up, Diane quickly moves into the new space she's created and powers up the empty lane.

Usually when you are dribbling, you are moving the ball forward. But there are times when you need to back away from the defense to encourage them to take off the pressure. When backing up while dribbling, it's important to not stand up. Keep your head forward and knees bent—so you can move forward again quickly if an opening occurs. And by staying low you are in a better position to protect the ball.

DRIBBLING CHECKLIST

- Keep your head up.
- Stay in your basketball stance—knees bent, back straight, leaning slightly forward.
- Practise each move with both your strong hand and your weak hand.
- The pads of your fingers are the most sensitive parts of your hand. The more you spread your fingers, the more space on the ball your fingers cover, and the more control you have.
- Your non-dribbling hand should protect the ball.

Dribbling Drill

Zach stays in his basketball stance as he dribbles a ball in each hand.

Two-ball dribbling, with one hand low and one high, adds a further challenge.

Remember: the best way to become a better dribbler is to dribble a ball everywhere you go—in the street, on grass, in the snow, at the beach. It's also important to be equally skilled with both hands. And if you can handle two balls at once, and at high speed, it will be so much easier when you only have one. So when you are in the gym, practise this two-ball dribbling series:

1 Stand in one spot in your basketball stance and dribble two balls simultaneously—one with each hand.
2 Move up the court, dribbling a ball with each hand.
3 Stand in one spot in your basketball stance and dribble a ball with each hand, alternating one high and one low.
4 Move up the court, dribbling a ball with each hand, alternating one high and one low.

PASSING

STRONG PASSING makes a basketball game move quickly and is key to a strong offense. It is also one of the least-practised skills. Passing can be used to avoid pressure, to move the defense, to control the tempo of the game, and, most important, to put a teammate in a better position to score. Remember: not all passes lead directly to the basket, and sometimes a simple pass is the most effective.

Accuracy and timing are important for good passing. A bad pass never helps your team—a bad pass to a well-placed shooter means she or he won't catch the ball *or* score. A bad pass can also be intercepted and result in a turnover. Possession is key—as long as your team has the ball, your opponents can't score.

"Ask me to play, I'll play. Ask me to shoot, I'll shoot. Ask me to pass, I'll pass. Ask me to steal, block out, sacrifice, lead, dominate—anything. But it's not what you ask of me. It's what I ask of myself."

< **LEBRON JAMES**

Practise passing to both moving and stationary players. Once you've mastered proper passing techniques, continue to work on increasing the quickness of your release and the ball's speed.

Two-Hand Chest Pass

Diane's hands are on either side of the ball, with her thumbs pointing at her chest. She takes a step forward to get power behind her pass.

She follows through with her arms extended and her fingers following the ball

PRO TIP The chest pass is called that because it's thrown from the chest. But don't throw the ball to the receiver's chest—throw it to where that player wants to receive it. It's your job to know where each player wants to catch the ball and to understand when *not* to pass to a specific player.

The two-hand chest pass is the most common and effective pass. If you have two hands on the ball, you will be stronger and have more control. Use this pass when you have a direct line between you and a teammate. But remember: this pass can be thrown with accuracy, but is difficult to make if a defender is in the way. Sometimes you will need to dribble to create some space.

- Get into your basketball stance, with your hands on either side of the ball. Your thumbs are directly behind and slightly under the middle of the ball, pointing at your chest. Your elbows should be shoulder-width apart, with the ball close to your chest. This gives you the most power and puts you in a position to do more than just pass if needed or if you have the opportunity.

- Take a step forward as you pass, rotating your hands under the ball to produce spin. A strong follow-through with your hands means your arms are extended, your palms are facing out, and your thumbs are down.

Bounce Pass

Zach uses a hard, sharp bounce to get the ball up into Gord's hands.
The ball hits the floor two-thirds of the way to the receiver.

The bounce pass is useful for avoiding the hands of a defender. But remember: it is slower than a chest pass because the ball slows down as it hits the floor. This might give a defender a chance to intercept, so the key is to get the ball up off the floor and into the hands of the receiver as sharply and accurately as possible. This pass is often used to get the ball into the post—where your teammate is waiting.

- The hand-and-arm technique is the same as for the two-hand chest pass, but this time the ball is bounced off the floor. Since the ball loses speed after it hits the floor, it must bounce closer to the receiver—ideally, two-thirds of the distance between the passer and the receiver.

PRO TIP Before you make a bounce pass, fake a high pass to move the defender's hands up and create an open lane.

Two-Hand Overhead Pass

Daniel is ready to use his wrists to make a quick throw over the heads of his defenders.

He follows through with his arms and hands to make sure the ball gets to his target.

PRO TIP Fake a chest or bounce pass before making an overhead pass, to move the defender's arms down. Use a short, snappy fake and keep the ball close to your core so that you can get it up and over your head quickly—and make the real pass before the defenders react and get their hands up into the passing lane.

To keep the ball away from defenders, throw the ball up and over their heads with an overhead pass. Remember: the most common mistake is to stand up straight and reveal your plan. Even if you know you want to use an overhead pass, keep the defense thinking that you might make a different move.

Also, use this pass when your teammate is asking for the ball up high or when a smaller defender has his or her hands down. The motion is similar to a soccer throw-in, except it's done more explosively. Remember: this pass avoids the traffic of hands and feet, but, once you commit, it is difficult to change your mind and make any other move.

- From your basketball stance, throw the ball with two hands from just above your forehead. Your hands should never go behind your head. Use a quick, strong flick of your wrists to give the pass speed—you need strong wrists because the ball must be thrown hard, with little or no arc. Your follow-through will leave your palms facing out and your thumbs pointing down.

Push Pass

Dustin steps past his defender to create an open lane.

He "pushes" the ball off of his inside hand, to his receiver.

Use the push pass when a defender is between you and your target, preventing you from making a two-handed pass. Be in your basketball stance, and keep the ball in both hands for as long as possible.

- Step to one side of your defender and lean past the defender's body. As you create a lane beside your defender, your outside hand will push the ball off your inside hand and over to the receiver. Step past the defender as you release the ball.

- This is called the "push pass" because, instead of winding up, you push the ball out of one hand with the other. The ball is pushed from your shoulder, and the follow-through leaves your arm fully extended in a straight line toward your target.

PRO TIP The push pass can also be a bounce pass. The most important thing is to have control, and to keep two hands on the ball for as long as you can.

One & Two, Down & Through

Dustin gets Jordan's hands up with two quick overhead fakes.

He moves his defender's hands down as he fakes a bounce pass.

He passes the ball past Jordan's ear and through the window.

PRO TIP If you make long, exaggerated fakes, you lose quickness and the defense will have time to recover. The further the ball is from your core, the less strength you have. Keep all fakes short, quick, and tight to the body.

Some coaches always say to fake a pass before you make a pass. This moves the defender's hands, and allows you to create a passing lane. Then you can deliver the ball where and when it is supposed to be delivered. This fake-and-pass sequence involves a quick combination of fakes that forces defenders to move their hands and therefore open up a passing window. You don't always have to use the one and two, down and through—you can use any combination of fakes—but this is one of the best.

- The "one and two" are two quick fakes of an overhead pass; the "down" is a fake of a bounce pass, followed by a real pass past the ear of the defender—"through" the window. The idea is to move the defender's hands up with the overhead fakes, then down with the bounce pass, creating a window to pass the ball through. Remember: make your fakes quick and concise. If they are over-exaggerated you will not be able to bring the ball back to your core where you have the most strength, control, and quickness.

Baseball Pass

Daniel steps forward to get more strength behind his pass.

He follows through, pointing directly at his target.

The baseball pass is a one-handed move that requires the same technique used to throw overhand in baseball. It is a powerful pass that can cover long distances. Use it to make a full-court pass to a player far away. A successful baseball pass can lead to a fast break or reach a player who has started a run down the floor. Use caution, though, because it's hard to be accurate with this pass, and it's an easy one for a speedy defender to pick up.

- Keep the ball in two hands for as long as possible. Turn your body sideways to the target. To create enough power for this longer throw, step toward your target with the foot that is opposite to your throwing hand, and use your leg strength. Throw the ball with one hand from beside your ear. Follow-through is important—your hand should end up pointed directly at your target.

- Make sure the ball is thrown with enough force that it arcs over the defenders, but don't throw it so high that you lose time and the defense is able to get under the pass and to your receiver.

- If your receiver is moving, throw the ball far enough ahead so that he or she can run under the ball and catch it.

PRO TIP The baseball pass is a great way for an in-bound player to take the ball out of bounds after a basket has been scored. If your teammate is open down the floor, the baseball pass will allow you to deliver the ball quickly.

Sidearm & Behind-the-Back Passes

Daniel stretches out to create a lane and throws the ball around his defender.

Jordan avoids a one-on-one with Zach by moving the ball behind his back to Gord.

PRO TIP The sidearm and behind-the-back passes are difficult for younger or smaller players, who might not have enough strength in their hands. You have to hold the ball in one hand for a long time. You are also holding the ball away from your core, which means that you have less control.

SIDEARM PASS Use the sidearm pass when a defender is directly between you and your teammate. This can be an effective pass, but it is a one-handed throw, so you will lose some accuracy and strength.

- Extend the ball away from your body and use the length of your arm to create space. Cup the ball in one hand, then throw it *around* the defender. Practise with a defender directly in front of you, and try to hit a target behind him or her. Use a spot on the wall as your target.

- You should be able to make a sidearm pass with either hand, so that you can move to both sides of your defender.

BEHIND-THE-BACK PASS Sometimes you are one-on-one with a defender and the only way to make a pass is to throw the ball from behind your back. This pass takes lots of strength, and is difficult to use for a long-distance throw. It's also hard to stop a one-handed pass once you've started. Remember: the behind-the-back pass is flashy, but also risky, because it can easily lead to a turnover.

- Move the ball from in front of your body to one side, and hold it with the hand on that side. Then throw the ball behind your back, following through by pointing at your target.

Passing Drills

Morgan's chest pass to Diane is released at the same time as Diane's bounce pass to Morgan.

Zach and Dustin add a third ball for an extra challenge, keeping all three balls in motion.

TWO-BALL PASSING Two players, each with one ball, stand 7 to 10 feet (2 to 3 metres) apart. Player 1 makes a bounce pass to player 2, who immediately makes a chest pass to player 1. Both players release their balls at the same time and catch them at chest height. The balls should be passed again as soon as they are caught.

THREE-BALL PASSING Player 1 starts with two balls, one in each hand. Player 2 has one ball, in his or her right hand. Player 1 throws the ball from his or her right hand to player 2's left hand, then passes the ball from his or her left hand to right hand. Player 2 throws the ball at player 1's left hand, which is now empty. Keep all three balls in the air and constantly moving.

PASSING CHECKLIST
- Always direct the ball to the receiver's target hand.
- Keep the ball in both hands for as long as possible.
- Stay in your stance and step toward your target as you throw.
- Follow through with your arms, hands, and fingers.

PROGRESSIONS

TWO-BALL
- Switch, so that the player doing the chest pass does the bounce pass and vice versa.
- Make the passes while shuffling sideways up the court.
- Have a coach direct you to switch passes and/or change directions.
- Move further apart and make quicker passes.

THREE-BALL
- Move up and down the court, passing and shuffling at the same time.

Catching

 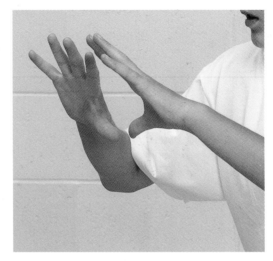

Dustin is in his basketball stance with his body facing the net, his hands creating a target and his eyes on the ball.

A good pass is only good if it can be caught—being able to catch is as important as being able to throw a good pass. Strong basketball players are always ready to receive the ball. Receiving a pass will get you into position to move the ball up the court, or maybe even to take a shot. It's easy to spend your time worrying about passing and shooting. But don't forget how important it is to know how to catch the ball too.

Remember: preparation is key. Your whole body must be prepared to catch the ball. Your feet face the basket and you are in your basketball stance. Your hands are up, your thumbs are together, and your fingers are spread. Help the teammate who is throwing to you by providing a target away from the hands of the defending player.

- Catch the ball between your shoulders and just under your chin. If you have to, reach for the ball with your hands *and* arms while stepping toward the ball. Catch it with the pads of your fingers, with your elbows bent, so that you can cushion fast, hard passes. Watch the ball right into your hands, and secure it by bringing it close to your body. This gives you the best chance to make your next move—another pass, a dribble, or a shot.

Diane helps her teammate by providing a target away from her defender's hands.

Diane reaches for the ball with both arms…

…then brings it in close to her chest, where she can protect it.

- If catching the ball in the post, you probably have a defender in your face or on your back. Provide a target by catching the ball away from the defender. For example, if the defender is leaning on your right shoulder, use your left hand as the target. Extend your left arm with your hand wide open, to create more distance from the defender. Make sure you are in a stance that will hold the defender away. Remember: catch the ball with two hands whenever possible, even if you are providing a target with one hand.

- Follow the ball with your eyes—from your teammate's hands right into your hands.

- Make a target with your hands. Spread your fingers and hold your hands in front of your chest—with your elbows bent so that you can absorb the pass.

- If you have to catch the ball outside your core, get it into your body, chest high, as fast as possible, so that you immediately become an offensive threat.

- Catch the ball with your knees bent, feet facing the basket, so that you will be prepared for your next move.

PRO TIP   Even if you provide a good target, not every pass will make it to your hands. Always be prepared to move to receive a bad or redirected throw.

SHOOTING

SHOOTING HOOPS and getting the ball into the basket is what basketball is all about. The greatest scorers in the game may not all have the same shooting form, but you can be sure they have all practised thousands of shooting variations and repetitions. Practise shooting with your team-mates and when no one else is around. Start every practice by standing under the basket and doing 5 minutes of form shooting. This warms up your shooting muscles and reminds your body and mind of the proper shooting motion.

"To be a good shooter, you have to shoot all the time. Inside the gym or outside on the pavement, you have to do it more than anyone else. It's all about repetition. Somebody somewhere is still practising! That's my motivation."
< **ANDREA BARGNANI**

Form Shooting

Dustin faces the basket with his elbow directly under the ball at a 90-degree angle. His left hand supports the ball, which is resting on the finger-pads of his shooting hand.

Dustin's arm is extended up, directing the ball into the basket. Form-shooting repetitions train your muscles into the proper technique.

PRO TIP Keep your eyes on the target. Pick a spot just over the front part of the rim and make the ball land there. If you hit that exact spot, the ball's momentum will carry it forward and into the basket. Remember: if you pick a spot on top of the rim, you need a good arc to make the ball land there.

Form shooting is a disciplined practice of repeated shots and the best way to train your muscles to remember proper technique. Practise form shooting 1 or 2 feet (a half-metre) from the basket. Players often practise too far from the basket and never develop proper technique.

- Stand in your basketball stance with your feet facing the basket and your weight on your toes. Your shooting-arm elbow is bent, with your forearm and bicep at a 90-degree angle, your elbow directly under the ball. Spread the fingers of your shooting hand, and rest the ball on the pads of your fingers, not the palm of your hand. Your index finger and middle finger should split the middle of the ball. Your wrist should be bent so that the ball can sit on this one hand without the support of the other. The other hand holds the ball in proper shooting position.

- Imagine that you are in a tube and have to shoot the ball up and out. First, move your shooting-arm elbow up, then extend your arm. If your arm extends too far forward, there will be no lift and the ball will release with no arc. Release the ball just before your arm reaches full extension. Remember: as the ball leaves your hand, roll your fingers under it to create the spin that will keep it moving in a straight line. Hold the follow-through until after the ball leaves your hand—show the ball where to go.

Jump Shot

Zach will release while he's still moving up, to give the ball upward momentum. His elbow is bent at 90-degrees and he supports the ball with both hands for as long as possible.

The jump shot is the same shot you practise in form shooting, except that you jump and then release the ball while you're still in the air. Use a jump shot if you are far from the basket and need extra height to reach the net, or if a defender is closing in and you need more time and space to get your shot away.

- Your legs are in motion at the same time that you begin your elbow lift and your movement upward. Your knees are bent, and as your legs straighten up, your feet leave the floor. You want to land back on the same spot you jumped from.

- Shoot the ball when you are on your way up. If you shoot at the peak of your jump, by the time you release the ball you will already be on your way down, which means you will have lost your upward momentum.

PRO TIP Effective shooting is about having the right touch and a feel for the ball. The best shooters in the game practise and perfect their technique, and then they do repetition after repetition. To become the best shooter, practise shooting more than everyone else.

Catch-and-Shoot: Standing

Daniel faces the basket, making a target for the ball, ready to move into shooting position.

In one motion, he's set to take a shot.

You already know how important it is to be in your basketball stance. But this is particularly important for a standing catch-and-shoot, when you need to turn neatly from receiving the ball to scoring a basket.

• Your feet are facing the basket, with your weight on your toes. Your knees are bent. Your hands are providing a target in front of your shoulders, with your fingers spread. And if you prepare like this, *before* you receive the ball, a good passer can get the ball right into your hands.

• After you receive the ball, your hands should immediately move to shooting position, with one hand under the ball and the other on the side of it as a guide. You shoot in one motion, leading with an elbow lift just as you did in form shooting.

Catch-and-Shoot: Off a Screen

Zach creates a perfect screen for Jordan, who moves into position to catch the ball.

He pivots on his inside foot until he is facing the basket…

… and in one motion, he's ready to shoot.

Good defenders don't leave you wide open and don't make it easy for you to catch-and-shoot. So, one way to lose a defender is to come off a screen. A "screen" is when a teammate plants her or his feet, then stands perfectly still, forcing the defender to run into him or her or change paths. This creates time and space for you to make your shot. Remember: move shoulder-to-shoulder past your teammate, so that you don't allow space for the defender to sneak through.

- As you come off the screen, ready to catch the ball, be prepared to take a shot. If you have the space to shoot, plant your inside foot—the one closest to the basket—and pivot until the other foot swings into place, facing the basket.

- Practise your pivot on both sides of the floor, so that you are comfortable using both feet. Repetitions are helpful. You should always have the proper stance and be facing the basket when catching the ball.

PRO TIP Your hands should always be up when you come off a screen. Your body should be low, not only for acceleration but also for making your shot.

Shooting off the Dribble

Zach's final bounce is fast and hard—to get the ball high.

He takes one long step to get away from his defender, keeping control of the ball.

He's in perfect position to make a jump shot.

PRO TIP   Use a quick dribble toward the basket to force your defender to back up. As the defender retreats to cover your drive, stop quickly and shoot the ball. The dribble gives you space to get the shot away.

Sometimes you have to dribble to get past a defender or to create space to get your shot away. Shooting off a dribble can be difficult if you don't have control of the ball or if you haven't planted your feet after the dribble to get balanced.

- If you are in your basketball stance you can get to the dribble quickly. The last dribble before you shoot should be a little harder and higher, so that you get into the ready position fast. Use the time when the ball is coming back up off the floor to prepare.

- To use the dribble to create space, you need to be able to move right or left. Also, your bounce should be as long as possible, without compromising your stance or balance. The further you can get from the defender, the more time you have for your shot. But it doesn't help if you are off balance and take a bad shot.

Layup

Zach keeps the ball close to his body as he pushes off with his left leg and drives up with his right.

He protects the ball with his left hand for as long as possible …

… and directs it softly to the backboard and into the net.

The layup is the conclusion of a drive to the basket. It's also one of the easiest shots to make in practice. But in a game with varying speeds, aggressive defenders, and different angles, it can be one of the trickiest.

- If you are shooting a right-handed layup, take the final step of your drive with your left leg, then launch yourself upward with your left foot. To get maximum height, drive your right knee up as your left foot pushes off. Keep two hands on the ball and hold it tight to your body until you get close to the basket. Keep the ball in both hands as long as possible, particularly if you are in traffic.

- When you're ready to shoot, extend your right arm fully while your left arm drops, for balance. The higher you jump and the faster you get to the rim, the better your chances of beating the defender.

- The layup shot should be soft, but it is difficult to transfer speed and momentum into a gentle shot. But if you don't transfer your forward momentum and shoot with too much force, the ball will bounce hard off the backboard. So use your guide hand to soften the release. And use the square on the backboard as a target. Every shot that softly hits this square should find its way into the basket.

PRO TIP Keep your release hand under the ball, with your fingers behind it. The last thing touching the ball are the pads of your fingers, where you have the most sensation. With practice, you'll learn how to make the release softer or even change the arc, depending on where the defense is.

Free Throw

Dustin's knees are bent, his back straight. His muscles remember the motion from his form-shooting practices.

He follows through with his arms and fingers, directing the ball into the net.

PRO TIP Make a practice shot with an imaginary ball before the referee gives you the real ball. This allows your body to rehearse the exact same motion you are about to perform. See the ball going in, and have a positive feeling before you even get the ball in your hands.

Develop a free-throw routine and follow it every time. The free throw is the only shot that is exactly the same in practice as it is in a game. There are no defenders, the distance is always the same, and you can take your time to prepare.

- As always, you start in your basketball stance. Your free throw should also be the same as your form shooting. Each and every time you practise, review all of the form-shooting points.

- Bounce the ball a couple of times before throwing it, to get a feel for the ball. Keep your eye on your target, not the ball. Breathe, to relax your mind and body. Concentrate on the shot.

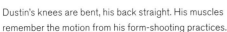

SHOOTING CHECKLIST
- Practise form shooting over and over, so that the motion becomes natural.
- Keep your weight on your toes and your knees bent.
- Your elbow under the ball should be at a 90-degree angle.
- Hold the ball on the pads of your fingers.
- Be ready and loaded to shoot even before you catch the ball.
- Practise catching and turning into the shot from both sides of the floor.
- Always follow through.

Shooting Drill

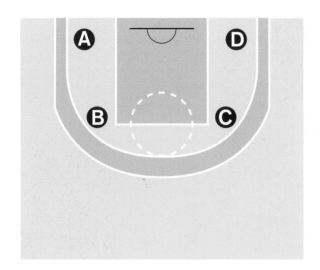
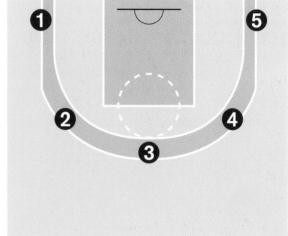

300-SHOT INDIVIDUAL WORKOUT

Make a score sheet for yourself that you can copy for repeated workouts.

- Warm up with 10 free throws and record your score. Make 25 shots from spot A. Sprint for the rebound and return to spot A without travelling. Record the number of successful shots.

- Shoot 10 more free throws, and record your score. Then repeat the shots-and-rebound routine at spot B. Then, repeat the entire drill at spots C and D. Finish with a final set of 10 free throws. Record your total score out of 150 shots.

- Next, move to spot 1. Throw the ball to yourself, catch it and shoot. Sprint for the rebound and run back to the spot. Repeat 10 times. Then fake a shot, dribble once, stop hard, and take a shot (called a "pull up"), going left 5 times. Then fake a shot, dribble once, and pull up going right 5 times. Record your score out of 20 shots from spot 1. Shoot 10 free throws, then repeat the entire drill, including free throws, from spot 2, 3, 4, and 5. Record your total score out of 150 shots.

FT	/ 10
A	/ 25
FT	/ 10
B	/ 25
FT	/ 10
C	/ 25
FT	/ 10
D	/ 25
TOTAL	**/ 150**

1	/ 20
FT	/ 10
2	/ 20
FT	/ 10
3	/ 20
FT	/ 10
4	/ 20
FT	/ 10
5	/ 20
FT	/ 10
TOTAL	**/ 150**

TOTAL	**/ 300**

PLAYING DEFENSE

DEFENSE IS half the game of basketball. The best defensive teams always have five players on the court who are as focused on defending their net as they are on shooting the ball. The player on the ball is the most active defender, but the off-ball defenders are equally important.

Offensive players have an advantage because they can choose when they want to move and where to. Defensive players have to react to offenders. The defenders' objective is to force a turnover—through a bad pass or violation—or to put the offenders in a position where they can take only poor shots. Prevent offensive players from getting close to the basket, and you decrease their chances to score.

Of course, the best defensive play is to not let your player get the ball. But good team defense depends on all four players who are *not* guarding the ball being ready to help if the player guarding the ball gets beat.

"I try to play the same all the time. I'll play hard if I play for five minutes or five seconds. If I start or come off the bench, I will play hard. I will play tough and I will play aggressively."
< **MANU GINOBILI**

Defensive Stance

Jordan digs for the ball with his right hand and discourages the pass with his left. His knees are bent, he's well-balanced, and he's ready to move in any direction.

The defensive stance is the same one you use for shooting, dribbling, and passing, except you don't have the ball. Your feet should be slightly more than shoulder-width apart. Your knees are bent, your butt down. One foot is slightly ahead of the other, to provide balance and enable you to move quickly. One hand is down, palm up and digging, to stop the offender from crossing the ball over. The other hand is up, to discourage passes. Your fingers are spread, to cover as much of the ball as possible and to deflect a pass or shot. The result: a stance that gives you balance and helps you change position as quickly as possible, eliminating your offenders' options. Remember: dig and discourage.

Rather than waiting to react to an offensive player, try to force that player to move in a particular direction. Put your right hand and foot forward a half-step, and force the offender to go to his or her right hand. Forcing players to their weak side can lead to a turnover or limit their options for plays.

Defensive Slide

Dustin's off-balance stance and passive hands allow Jordan to easily move past.

Dustin's arms and hands limit Jordan's options for passing or dribbling, and his wide stance means he's well balanced and ready to move or pivot in any direction.

The defensive slide is the best technique for staying with an offensive player. Stay low and in your defensive stance, so that you can quickly react to the offender's movements.

- When sliding, your ball-side hand is up and discouraging passes. Your other hand is digging, to prevent a crossover dribble while you stay ready to steal the ball or pick up a deflection. Step or slide sideways, keeping contact with the floor. Make sure your feet never come together or cross over, which could throw you off balance. Short, choppy slides help you stay low in your stance. Don't release into a standing position.

- If the offender changes direction, you change direction as well. Use your elbow to swing and make a quick 45-degree pivot, which should put you in the perfect position to defend in the other direction. The hand that was discouraging passes now becomes the hand that discourages the crossover dribble. If your left foot was forward, forcing the offender to the left, now your right foot should be up.

PRO TIP Decide how to defend depending on the strengths and weaknesses of the player you are guarding. If the player is quick, back off a half-step. If you're facing a great shooter, you need to be up close. If the offender has a weak left hand, force him or her to go in that direction.

On-the-Ball Defense

Diane is in her defensive stance, ready to stop Morgan from dribbling or passing.

When Morgan commits to an overhead pass, Diane moves in close to block.

When guarding on the ball, stay in a line between the offensive player and the basket. If the offender stops dribbling and is holding the ball, move in close and keep your hands active, to deflect a pass. If the offender has not dribbled and is in a basketball stance, be prepared for a shot, a dribble, or a pass.

- When guarding a player who has an opportunity to dribble, be in your defensive stance and ready to react. Your hands should be active and discouraging passes and shots, forcing the offender to move in the direction you want. One of your hands is up and in the passing lane, ready to block a shot. The other hand is down and digging at the ball. Positioning your hands like this also creates balance, because if both hands are up, it is difficult to use your defensive slide.

- If you can make the offender pick up the ball or lose the dribble, move in close and trace or cover the ball with both hands. Keep your knees bent, so that if a pass is made, you recover quickly.

Denying the Pass

Jordan is two-thirds of the way between the ball and his player, with one arm in the lane to discourage the pass.

When the player you are guarding is in a better scoring position than the player with the ball, make it impossible for your player to receive a pass. Force your opponent to miss the pass or to catch it away from the basket, and you have done a good job.

- How far the ball handler is from your player determines how far from your player you need to be. Position yourself two-thirds of the way between the ball and your player. Be in the defensive stance, with one foot and one hand in the passing lane. Look straight down your extended arm so that you can see both the ball and your player with your peripheral vision. Your thumb should be down and your palm open, so that you can discourage or knock down a pass. As your player tries to get open, you are going to move as well, keeping your top foot and hand in the line of the pass.

PRO TIP If you can't see both the ball and the player you are guarding, you are not in the correct defensive position. You will have to adjust your feet and location.

Weak-Side Defense

Dustin and Jordan each form a triangle with their player and the ball so they can keep their eyes on the ball and are ready to react if their player makes a move.

Weak-side defense means that the ball is in the hands of an opponent—but not the player you are guarding. Remember: always be able to see both your player *and* the ball, so that you can help quickly if your teammate gets beat or if your player makes a move to the basket.

- Be in your defensive stance. Form a triangle—with yourself, the player with the ball, and the player you are guarding. Then, with your hands in a pistol position, point at the ball with one hand and at your player with the other. Drop back, so that you can see both the ball and your player—the size of your triangle depends on the distance between them. If your player is close to the ball but not in possession, shrink the triangle, so that you can use your hand in the passing lane. The farther the ball is from your player, the more you move away from your player and up the line, between your player and the ball.

Closing Out & Challenging the Shot

Matthew gets in position and points his pistols at the ball and at the player he's guarding.

If you are guarding off the ball and a pass is made to your player, you have to get there as fast as possible. This is the "close-out." With a proper close-out, you get to your player and get in your stance, prepared to challenge the shot, before your player even receives the ball.

You should already be in your defensive stance, in a triangle with the player you are guarding and the player with the ball. Point your pistols, and make sure your position allows you to see both players and the ball. If the ball is thrown to your player, you start the close-out. You will have to go from your basketball stance into a full sprint and then a quick stop, and be back in your stance. You want to be in control so that you can force the offender's play. But be careful: running toward the player you are guarding in a full sprint puts you in a vulnerable position, because your momentum is taking you in the opposite direction to the direction that player wants to move.

PRO TIP When closing out, judge how close to get by evaluating the player's skills. If the player is a great shooter, close out further back, to take the shot away. If the player is a poor shooter, close out short, to guard against the drive.

Closing Out & Challenging the Shot

When Dustin releases the ball, Matthew starts his close-out. He sprints to his player …

… and gets his arms up, ready to block Ethan's pass or shot.

PRO TIP When challenging a shot, it is important not to let your feet leave the floor until the shooter's feet leave the floor. Otherwise, you could pick up a foul or take yourself out of position for boxing out.

- Since you were in a good defensive position when you were off the ball, you know when and where the ball is being passed. Get to your player and be in control as fast as possible. The more ground you can cover while the ball is in the air, the closer you will be when your player receives it. Sprint two-thirds of the distance between you and the offender. At the two-thirds point, use short, choppy steps to slow your forward momentum. Throw both arms in the air, and get in a proper stance, ready to respond to a pass, a shot, or the drive.

- When defending on the ball, keep pressure on the offender. With good pressure, you can force the pass to be thrown higher, so that the ball takes longer to get to the target, allowing the player closing out to cover more ground and maybe even get a steal. It takes more than one player to defend. If all five players work together, you will be a strong defensive team.

Defense Drill

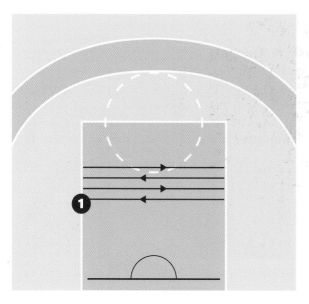 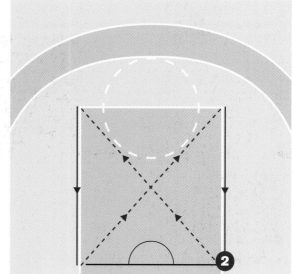

1 Get in your defensive stance, facing the baseline. Start with one foot on the side of the free-throw lane. Then slide across to the other side of the lane and back as many times as you can in 30 seconds. Stay in your stance, and remember: your feet should never come together.

2 Starting on one side of the lane at the baseline, slide diagonally across the free-throw lane to the opposite side of the lane at the free-throw line. Sprint straight down the lane to the baseline, then slide to the opposite side at the free-throw line. See how many sets you can do in 30 seconds. This drill will improve your lateral quickness and conditioning.

- - - - - - - - - - - - - - - - -

DEFENSE CHECKLIST
- Stay in your defensive stance, whether you are guarding on or off the ball.
- Always be in a position where you can see both your player and the ball.
- Use your hands and fingers to point at the ball and at your player.
- Force the offense to do what you want them to do.
- Be ready to read and react to the offensive players' moves.

- - - - - - - - - - - -

RE
BOUNDING

GOOD REBOUNDING wins basketball games. You need the ball to score, and the more opportunities you have to score, the better your chances of winning a game. Every time the ball is shot, it becomes a free ball. Strong rebounding can regain possession of the ball for your team or take possession away from the opposition.

The offensive rebound is when your team misses a shot and you retrieve the ball to give your team another chance to score. The defensive rebound is when you secure the ball after the other team has attempted a shot and missed.

Positioning, jumping ability, and strength are important, but rebounding is mostly about instinct and effort. The keener your instincts, the more you can anticipate where the ball will be next and the faster you can chase it down. You have to work hard, be aggressive, and be willing to be bumped around.

"Get stronger, keep practising everyday, follow your dream and one day it will come true."
< YAO MING

Offensive Rebounds

Zach uses "the swim" to get his arms up and over Daniel's, and ends up in front of his defender.

Daniel and Zach are both looking for the rebound.

If you are on offense, there is usually a defender between you and the basket when your team shoots the ball. The defender tries to keep you from getting close to the basket by boxing you out. Good offensive rebounders find a way to get past the defender to the inside position and regain possession for their team.

- You have several ways to get around a defender. Plan where you want to go. If the ball is shot from one side of the floor, it's likely that the rebound will bounce to the other side. How do you get there quickly? Fake one way, then change direction fast to be the first player to that spot.

- Remember: the farther from the basket the shot is taken, the farther away the ball will bounce. Position yourself according to the shot. For example, it doesn't make sense to fight to get under the basket after a three-point shot.

Movement & Positioning

Daniel makes contact to keep Zach out … but Zach uses the contact to spin around.

Zach ends up in front of his defender—and in a better position to capture the rebound.

THE SWIM Sometimes a defender will make contact to keep you from getting in a good position. If contact is made, don't stop working and don't stop pursuing the ball. A couple of techniques are effective. The first is "the swim." Bring your arm over the shoulder of the defensive player, as if you were swimming. Once your arm is over the shoulder, use your body to hold the defender to one side—so that you are beside the defensive player and have an equal chance to grab the rebound.

THE SPIN The other technique is "the spin." The defender will be looking for the ball and trying to make contact. Use the contact to spin and get beside the defender. Use an arm or shoulder to bump the defensive player, then roll so that you are back-to-back for a split second. Keep body contact during the spin. This allows you to get to the other side of the player trying to box you out—or even in front if you can spin quickly enough.

PRO TIP You have to decide when to pursue the offensive rebound. If your team doesn't end up with the ball, the other team is in a position to break and beat you down the floor. But if your team gets an offensive rebound, your chances of scoring right away are very good, since the defense will not be in a great position.

Defensive Rebounds

Daniel starts his box out, keeping his eyes on the ball and using his body to keep Zach from getting to the rebound.

He explodes up to the net and successfully pursues the ball …

… and secures it close to his body, under his chin.

Rebounding is the final stage of a good defensive effort in which you have forced your opponents to miss a shot. But the effort is wasted if the other team retrieves the rebound. The most common defensive rebound play is "boxing out," which means hitting offenders with your hip or butt, to redirect or slow them down in their pursuit. After you box out, you pursue: you chase, jump for, and secure the ball.

- You should already be in the ideal position between your player and the basket. The best way to box out is to pivot and spin into the offender. By making contact, you know where the player is, so you can keep your eyes on the ball. Stay low in your stance—if you stand up straight, you can lose your balance. Your hands are up and your elbows bent, since the ball can come off the rim very fast. Use your arms to hold off the offender and don't lean back—you need forward momentum.

- After you've made contact, pursue the ball. If you release too early, the offender will follow you and have a chance at the rebound. If you maintain contact too long, the ball may hit the floor. Predict when and where the ball will bounce off the rim, then release, exploding up with a jump. Catch the ball as high as you can with both hands. Land solidly, then secure the ball against your upper chest and hold it under your chin.

Rebound Drill

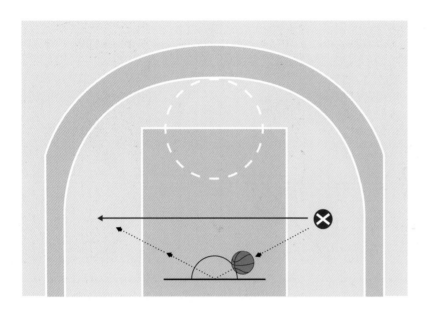

Start on one side of the lane about 10 feet (3 metres) from the basket.
Bounce the ball off the backboard directly above the rim, then chase
the ball and catch it as high up in the air as possible with both hands.
Your momentum should have you land just outside the lane on the opposite side. Repeat 10 times. This drill helps with conditioning, jumping,
and catching skills, as well as with proper technique for protecting the
ball after catching the rebound.

. . . .

REBOUND CHECKLIST
- Position yourself between the person you are guarding and the ball.
- Stay in your stance, so that you are strong and ready to pursue.
- Make contact, to discourage opponents from pursuing the ball.

. . . .

5 PLAYS THAT MAKE A DIFFERENCE

SOME MOVES and plays that seem minor can make the difference between possession of the ball and no possession—and even between winning or losing. Every player that wants to be good will work on the skills that we have talked about in this book. And like the fundamentals such as shooting and dribbling, small moves like getting open, setting good screens, and taking charges are the plays that help win games. If you think about and practise these plays, you will be a more valuable player and a better teammate.

As important as learning the skills is how you think about the game, and which moves become instinctive. For example, you should know by instinct how and when to save the ball. And a solid, well-positioned screen might give your player a better opportunity for a jump shot. These might be small plays, but they will make a difference.

"I'll do whatever it takes to win games, whether that's sitting on a bench waving a towel, handing a cup of water to a teammate, or hitting the game-winning shot."
< **KOBE BRYANT**

On Offense: Getting Open

Daniel's on offense. He moves in from the lane and plants his inside foot over Zach's.

He launches into an L-cut …

… and gets himself open to receive the ball.

When your team is on offense, work hard to keep yourself open so that your teammates can pass to you. The harder you work to get open, the more you decrease the chance of a defender intercepting a pass that is thrown to you. Where you are when you catch the ball determines how many options you have. If you receive the ball when you're too far from the basket, you may not be in the best scoring position.

PRO TIP Make a small fake before making your cut up the lane, to create a little separation from the defender. Bump and freeze the defender before making a hard cut to get open. The closer you get to the basket, the more options you have to make a shot or a pass to a teammate.

THE FAKE You should always be anticipating a pass and always ready to catch the ball. The defense will be trying to block or intercept the pass. Throw off your defender by faking a move in one direction, then going in the opposite direction. Make a hard cut to the open area where you want to receive the ball.

THE L-CUT Most of the time you want to receive the ball on the wing. When you're in the free-throw lane, make a little body contact with your defender and put your inside—or top—foot over the defender's top foot. Plant your foot, then push off hard at a 45-degree angle to the wing, making an L-shaped move, to get yourself clear and ready to receive a pass.

On Offense: One-on-One Play

Diane makes a quick series of fakes while keeping the ball secure in her core.

Diane fakes a shot, forcing Morgan to get her arms up …

…then quickly dribbles past her defender and to the basket.

Many times in a game you play one-on-one with a defender. Make sure you have the skills to get past the defense. You have to make a move or fake to clear a path to the basket or to get yourself into a better offensive position.

- When making a fake, keep the ball close to your core and in your power area, from your knees to your shoulders. If you fake outside this area, you lose strength, quickness, and time as you bring the ball back in to make your real move. Your core is the starting point for all your moves.

- From your core, you can also fake in several ways. Fake a shot by bringing the ball to one shoulder, forcing the defender to stand up. Fake a drive by moving the ball to either knee, making the defender back off. A pass fake opens up a passing lane. Or, move the ball within your core area, taking quick jab-steps to make the defender think you will drive past. Your goal is to make the defender react to a realistic fake. You then take advantage by moving into the open space and past the defense.

PRO TIP It's important to make every fake move as realistic as the real thing. Fakes have to be quick, precise, and tight to your body—don't waste time between making the fake move, forcing the defender to react, and making your real move.

On Offense: Setting Screens

Daniel sets a bad screen—he's taking up as little room as possible and is not in a ready stance.

Daniel in an effective screen—he's spread out, making himself as wide and as deep as possible. His knees are bent to absorb contact—and he's ready to react to the play.

Daniel sets a perfect screen, allowing Dustin to get open to receive a pass.

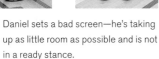

PRO TIP Setting a screen not only helps your teammate get open, but often the defender guarding the screener will move to help a teammate, and that leaves you open to get the ball—and maybe even a basket.

One of the best ways to help a teammate get open is to set a screen. You can set screens on the ball or for players trying to get open. But remember: as a screener, you are not allowed to move and you have to make yourself as big as you can. The goal is to make contact and free up your teammate from the player trying to guard.

- An effective screen is solid and takes up as much room as possible. Stand with your feet set and spread, at least shoulder width apart. Wide is better, but be careful to not stick out your legs—this isn't allowed. Bend your knees, so that you are able to absorb contact and so you are a deeper screen from front to back. Your width and depth are both important, because players will have to run around the screen. You want to take up space.

On Defense

Matthew has his eyes on his player and the ball.

When his teammate gets beat, Matthew moves in on Dustin and "takes a charge."

TAKING A CHARGE One of the best moves a defender has is "taking a charge." Stand, with your feet planted, directly in front of the offender who is trying to get to the basket. This forces the offender to make contact and costs a personal foul. It also stops the offense from getting to the basket and gives your team possession.

- The key is to anticipate where the offender is going. Beat the player to that spot and establish your position. Be willing to get hit and fall to the floor.

- Off-ball defenders can slide over to take a charge if a teammate gets beat.

SAVING THE BALL When the ball is going out of bounds, you usually want to knock it back into play so that your team gains or keeps possession.

- First, try to save the ball directly to a teammate. Second, save the ball into play as far away from your basket as possible, so that if the other team gets it, you can get back into play prepared to defend.

- Do not save the ball under the basket you're defending. If it's intercepted, that's two easy points for the opposition. It's better to take the ball out of bounds with you so the other team can't save it. This also gives your defense time to get reorganized.

PRO TIP When you take a charge, anticipate the contact and start to fall slightly before you get hit. This lessens the impact on your body. Bend your knees as you fall so that your butt is the first thing that hits the floor, then break your fall with your hands, elbows, and back, in that order.

CONCLUSION

THE BASICS: that's what pure basketball is all about. Sure, there are players who can dunk and make flashy plays that get on the TV highlight reels. But professional players, like the ones you see in this book, truly know and understand the fundamentals of the game. Steve Nash—a two-time NBA MVP—can't dunk a basketball. But he has practised and practised all of the basic skills. And now he is recognized as one of the best players in the world.

Too many players just want to have fun in games. This diminishes the importance of working on your skills. With this book, I hope that I have inspired you to practise, and provided drills and ideas to help you improve your game—by studying the basics, learning how to do them perfectly and at game speed, then incorporating them into game situations. But remember: don't just practise a few times here and there. *Practise the basics all the time.* That's how you will see the greatest improvement in your game. A commitment to the basics of basketball will make you a better player—and, like everything else in life, the more you put into it, the more you will get out of it.

And don't forget: always listen to the coach!

JAY TRIANO

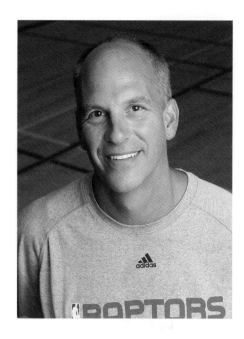

JAY TRIANO is Interim Head Coach with the NBA's Toronto Raptors. He was Assistant Coach of the USA-B Select Team in 2007, Head Coach at the NIKE Skills Academy (2006 and 2007), and Coach at the prestigious EURO CAMP in Treviso, Italy (2003–08).

Triano began his coaching ca reer at Simon Fraser University in Burnaby, British Columbia, where he was Head Coach from 1988 until 1995. In 1993–94, he was also Head Coach of the Canadian men's junior national team.

Triano played for the Canadian national team for 11 years (1978–88), was team Captain from 1981–88, and played for Canada at three Olympics (1980, 1984, 1988), serving as Captain for the last two. He was also Head Coach of the 2000 Canadian Olympic team, which finished with a 5–2 record in Sydney.

A member of the Canadian Basketball and Olympic Halls of Fame, Triano has also worked as a basketball analyst for TSN. He was a CBC Sports broadcaster for the Olympic Games in Athens in 2004 and Beijing in 2008.

In 2005, Jay Triano was given the Coach Mac Award. This honour, named after the late, legendary John B. McLendon, is given annually to a member of the Canadian basketball community who, through exemplary character and effort, has made a significant contribution to the sport of basketball while upholding the principles for which Coach Mac stood: honesty, integrity, competitiveness, and a love of the game.

The Basketball Basics Team

Advisors

CHRIS BOSH Toronto Raptors, three-time NBA All-Star

BRYAN COLANGELO President and General Manager, Toronto Raptors

KEITH D'AMELIO Strength and Conditioning Coach, Toronto Raptors

GREG FRANCIS Head Coach, Canada Basketball Development Team

KEVIN HANSON Head Basketball Coach, University of British Columbia

MIKE KATZ Head Basketball Coach, University of Toronto

JAMA MAHLALELA Coordinator of Basketball Development, Toronto Raptors

STEVE NASH Phoenix Suns, two-time NBA Most Valuable Player

Special thanks

STEPHEN McGILLIGAN Boys' Coach, South Delta Secondary School

JON LEE NSCA Certified Strength and Conditioning Specialist

STEPHEN "COACH" McGILLIGAN   **JON LEE**

Players

MORGAN BOURQUE   **DIANE DEWAR**   **JORDAN JONES**   **DANIEL JUTRAS**   **MATTHEW JUTRAS**

ZACH NICHOLLS   **GORD NICHOLSON**   **ETHAN SCOTT**   **DUSTIN TRIANO**